Contents

Prelude

Where do I start?

For anyone responsible for raising income for a charity or social enterprise, trying to work out where to start is always a problem.

Only once or twice have I had sufficient time to establish income growth strategies. Normally the atmosphere has been one of quietly suppressed panic, or if I've been really unlucky, open panic. This section assumes that you and your organisation are at least nervous about having enough money for the future and perhaps even the present. So if your hand is hovering above the panic button, start here.

We need to address your current situation first because:

- raising enough sustainable income takes time in terms of analysing, planning, experimenting and delivering. This strategic approach is what this publication is about

- if you are worried about survival, it is nearly impossible to concentrate on developing an income generating strategy while trying to meet short-term funding imperatives – or more bluntly – balancing the books

Prelude

A few questions

Question 1

Have you got enough money and other resources (such as volunteers and gifts in kind) to keep going for the next year or so?

If you have, then just make sure you are covering step 4 on the next page and then go to section 2: introduction.

Question 2

If you haven't enough money for the next year, then how bad is it and who is telling you this?

Because if someone who is generally optimistic is telling you things are bad, then you have a real problem, and short-term fundraising is unlikely to be the answer. If your organisation still has a budget shortfall of more than 25%-40% for the coming year and this is the third or fourth budget iteration, then the situation is bad. Unless you already have fundraising initiatives in place that have a high probability of success, then new income initiatives will not be the answer to your short-term needs.

Question 3

If things are that bad, what is the answer?

The only answer is cutting expenditure, for two reasons. First, unless you have significant reserves to tide you over, you will go bankrupt. Second, raising money when it is apparent that you cannot balance the books is virtually impossible. So cutting back needs to happen alongside other possible interventions such as loans. Your job is to raise some income fast, in parallel with any cutback process. This is covered under Question 4.

Information about loans for the Voluntary and Community Sector (VCS) can be found on NCVO's Sustainable Funding Project's web pages.

Question 4

What if there is a problem, but you believe it is exaggerated?

This implies you need to raise additional net income fairly soon or face needing to cut expenditure. Unless there is some new income in the pipeline, there is only one way I know in the short term – to persuade one or more existing supporters to give more. Any other methods usually have lead times of one or two years. That is too long for your board/committee who by that time will be grumbling to you, or, even worse, grumbling behind your back.

Question 5

How do I raise more from existing supporters?

The rest of this guide gives you tools and a framework to identify sources of income, target supporters, ascertain and meet their needs so that they will give you resources and, most importantly, keep on doing so year after year. But the purpose of the next four steps is to help those who need a quick fix to buy time to develop and implement a successful, sustainable income strategy.

How do I raise more money from existing supporters

Existing supporters come in all shapes and sizes.

Step 1: review where all your organisation's resources come from

The annual accounts/annual budget and the treasurer/head of finance will give you a picture of incoming resources, not just in terms of money, but also volunteer/pro bono contributions and contributions in kind (such as reduced rent, shared reception service, shared computer support etc).

Step 2: select those resource contributors who are most able to assist you in a crisis.

For example, if a trust is providing you with core funding (ie not tied to any particular activity) can you get specific additional help? If you share a receptionist with a host organisation, do they have any spare capacity that could be used to take on some work for your organisation? In your regular mailings to supporters could you insert an additional emergency appeal? Is the local authority or health authority currently commissioning services from you that could be expanded for an enhanced fee, especially towards the end of their financial year when there may be some underspend?

It is really worth working hard on these lines because it is so much cheaper, quicker and more effective to get more resources from an existing supporter than it is to find a new one. In business it is between five and ten times cheaper to retain and expand the purchasing of an existing customer than to find a new one.

Step 3: work out your ask.

It is crucial to use your knowledge of the customer (donor, customer, purchaser, commissioner etc) – in particular their needs, wishes and interests. You obviously need to frame your ask in language and terms that will appeal to them, not always in those that appeal to you. But you must be honest. If you say one thing and do another not only is that unethical, you will be caught out and you will lose a valuable supporter. Your ask also needs to be as concrete and graphic as you can manage. It may be very real to you but it is at one or two removes from your supporter and may not engage or grab them. So take your supporter out to show them your work in action; take along an eloquent beneficiary of your services to tell them what a difference you have made and show them your plans for the future.

Step 4: keep building your relationship with your supporter after their 'yes' decision (or even a 'no' one).

Many supporters complain that they only hear from a charity when it needs more money and that they feel used. Between asks, keep in touch and use a variety of approaches:

- invite them to your AGM as guests of honour and publicly acknowledge them on the day
- invite them to receptions hosted by your patron
- take photos of them with local dignitaries
- create service/activity open days and invite them again as guests of honour
- invite them to a board/committee meeting.

Consider inviting them to events of this nature approximately twice a year.

When you are short of immediate resources, this is an approach to take to achieve quick fundraising success. But **the purpose of the rest of this guide is to describe how a marketing approach can help you build and maintain a sustainable income for your cause and this is what we turn to now.**

Links
The Sustainable Funding Project's web pages on Loan finance:
www.ncvo-vol.org.uk /sfp/loans

Chapter 1

Introduction to Marketing for Sustainable Funding

This guide does something fairly unique, it applies commercial marketing to VCO income generation. If you have studied marketing before, you will know that it is not simply advertising, PR and selling. In the context of this publication marketing is the theory, framework and set of tools for:

Meeting the needs of your income providers, while staying focused on the objectives of your organisation.

Why is this important? First it is obvious that if a VCO does not meet the needs of its funders, they will cease to fund. But, in my experience, the majority of VCOs are poor to very poor at meeting the needs of funders. This is because they do not have the theory and tools they need to do this well.

If you know all about commercial marketing you will not need this publication, but if you do not, or need a refresher, please read on. I was trained in the commercial sector, and have spent over 30 years in the voluntary sector applying commercial marketing principles to non-profit income generation, service delivery and pressure group/campaigning. In this publication we are only dealing with income generation, but if you want the full picture you can read *Charity Marketing* (Bruce 2005).

So what kind of funding are we talking about? The Sustainable Funding Project (SFP) has developed a very useful *Income Spectrum* ranging from donations (Gift Economy) that can be used for any charitable purpose (on the left hand side) through increasingly restricted funding sources till we reach services/products sold in the open market on the right.

The Sustainable Funding Project at NCVO has several other useful resources to help you with the practical steps of increasing your income and these are listed at the end and are referenced throughout this publication.

Sustainable Funding: Across the Income Spectrum

Income options available to voluntary and community organisations

Donor	Funder	Purchaser	Consumer

Gift Economy

Philanthropic giving, voluntary donations, pure charity. Provides unrestricted income for an organisation to use at their discretion to further their charitable aims.

Grant Funding

Usually restricted funding provided to deliver specified outputs and/or mutually agreed outcomes. Grant funders are likely to want to monitor what is done with their investment and have clear expectations about what will be achieved.

Structured Market

Payment for goods or services according to the terms set out in a contract between an organisation and a third party purchaser, be it from the public, private or voluntary sectors.

Open Market

Within the overall realm of trading, the range of services and goods that can be sold is potentially endless. Some types of trading are undertaken purely to generate profit, while other types can also contribute to the delivery of an organisation's mission. Income generated in this way is unrestricted.

ASKING   EARNING

Different income types are accessed and managed in different ways and involve different relationships with the individual or organisation supplying the funds. As you move across the spectrum from left to right – from asking to earning – the level of expectation regarding what is received in return for the income increases.

Within the range of options there is enormous variety and possibility. Sustainable funding can involve all these income streams, or a more limited range – diversification across the spectrum, or if that is not possible or appropriate, within a particular stream.

The key to sustainability is knowing which streams are the right ones for your organisation to explore and how you can develop the capacity to be able to secure and manage them.

This guide does not cover all the differences between commercial and non-profit marketing but there is one that is crucial to income generation, in particular in the first three markets illustrated above:

- in commercial marketing the customer who pays is generally the one who consumes (eg you pay for a TV, which you then put in your house and watch)

- in non-profit income generation marketing, the customer (sometimes called stakeholder) who funds (eg donor, trust, commissioner) generally IS NOT the customer who consumes (ie the beneficiary – who might go under various names eg client, member, patient, student etc)

So here we have two different sets of customers who often have different sets of needs. Our causes (and our charitable status if we have it) demand that meeting beneficiary needs has precedence over meeting funder needs. I have met some fundraisers who argue that they can be equal but that is wrong (often legally so) and dangerous because it can lead to mission drift.

To complete the picture of non-profit customer groups I divide all people we have to serve into four groups:

- **beneficiaries**
- **supporters** (including donors, purchasers, commissioners etc)
- **stakeholders** (eg staff, trustees, representatives of beneficiaries etc)
- **regulators** (eg Charity Commission, Fundraising Standards Board, Local Authority, Gambling Commission etc).

The needs of all four groups have to be met if we are to do our work effectively.

But remember, to reach these **end** customer groups we normally have to work through intermediaries who also have needs and wishes that have to be met, eg to reach church goers you have to gain the help of the vicar; to reach company employees you have to work through company management and union leaders. So in these instances the managers, union leaders and religious leaders are **intermediary customers**.

Chapter 2

Deciding a thoughtful (Strategic) Expansion of Income

There are countless possibilities for raising additional income – so it is vital to think through:

- which efforts are likely to be most successful

- which successful efforts will strengthen our organisation in the medium term rather than blow us off course (mission drift) or leave us in the lurch (short-term funding that cannot be renewed)

- how we design our efforts to be as effective as possible

Much of this marketing thinking is common sense but there are stages and some analytical tools we can use that apply to all four of our markets – the gift economy, the grant economy, the structured market and the open market.

Stage 1: Marketing analysis

Which includes:

- market analysis
- Ansoff matrix
- SWOT (strengths weaknesses opportunities and threats) but concentrating on strengths analysis
- competitor analysis
- positioning
- segmentation.

Stage 2: Helping you choose which fundraising/income generation method to use

The choice between:

- The Gift Economy, Grants, Structured Market and Open Market, which includes choosing between legacies, trusts, major donors, direct mail, corporate, employee fundraising, local/community fundraising (street collections, door to door, raffles, fairs, shops), commissioning, trading etc.

Now if this list of stages makes you frustrated, there are two points to make:

- first if you are desperate for money now and do not have time to invest in a professional approach, the prelude gives you some ideas as to what you can do. When you have done it you can come back to this section.

- second, if you can't stand jargon or are impetuous and just want to get on with income generation, then move straight to the fundraising section, Stage 2. BUT before you start to act on the chosen method(s), do please consider Stages 1 and 3. Without Stages 1 and 3, I have seen many organisations come unstuck two or three years down the line. This is because they have chosen an unsuccessful method, or damaged their reputation, or have become over dependent on one source, or have suffered mission drift by simply chasing the money – the pitfalls are numerous and Stages 1 and 3 will help you avoid them.

Stage 3: Income generation product development using marketing theory

Comprising of:

- fundraising marketing mix (product, price, promotion, place, people, physical evidence, processes and philosophy)

- relationship marketing for sustainable income generation.

Stage 1: Marketing analysis

Marketing analysis helps you:

- choose the most promising pots of money to go after

- choose methods with which you are more likely to succeed and avoid superficially attractive methods, which are likely to fail

- identify the strengths in your organisation and your people, which will be valuable in fundraising

- find out what other charities or non-profits like you are doing with their fundraising

- understand what your supporters think about your organisation and identify the strengths you must protect and build on in your fundraising

- identify the kinds of people and organisations who are more or less likely to give to, or contract with, your organisation.

There is no particular order to the following activities, although it may be best to do the SWOT last so that you are already beginning to build a short list of expanded or new methods. SWOT helps you identify strengths and weaknesses to do some specific income development methods and thus get more realistic answers as to whether you have the knowledge and skills.

Market analysis

There are more categories/sources of income available than most people realise as can be seen from the table below. I am writing this in 2010 but I am certain that the main messages in the table below will be roughly the same up to 2020, namely that:

- one of the biggest resources for charities are **individuals** (through methods such as legacies, collecting tins, raffles, regular donations etc) and the **state** (eg local and national government and NHS grants and contracts)
- the other is **earned income** (eg from contracts, individual purchases such as disability aids or trading)
- the private sector provides only a very small proportion of charity income

Overleaf I use the NCVO *UK Civil Society Almanac* breakdown, which gives specific market sizes.

Chapter 2: marketing analysis

How do you compare to other organisations?

Voluntary sector income by size of organisation, from NCVO Almanac 2010 (%)

	Micro	Small	Medium	Large	Major	Total	Your organisation
Individuals (excluding legacies)	32.4	15.7	15.6	15.0	17.3	16.3	
Legacies	0.9	0.3	2.7	3.1	9.4	5.6	
Statutory sources (excluding National Lottery distributors)	4.1	9.3	16.3	12.3	6.8	10.4	
National Lottery distributors	2.0	1.4	2.7	1.8	0.7	1.5	
Voluntary sector	5.1	5.0	6.8	5.1	3.7	4.8	
Private sector	0.5	1.1	2.2	3.8	3.9	3.4	
Total voluntary income	**45.0**	**32.8**	**46.4**	**41.1**	**41.8**	**42.0**	
Individuals	30.4	32.1	17.5	15.6	11.1	14.9	
Statutory sources	1.4	12.9	18.9	25.6	30.5	25.7	
Voluntary sector	4.4	7.5	4.3	2.7	3.3	3.5	
Private sector	1.8	1.4	2.4	2.8	1.9	2.3	
Trading subsidiaries	0.0	0.1	1.3	3.2	3.1	2.6	
Total earned income	**38.1**	**53.9**	**44.4**	**50.0**	**49.9**	**49.1**	
Rent from property	0.0	0.8	2.0	2.3	0.7	1.5	
Dividends etc	5.6	8.5	5.7	4.9	6.5	5.9	
Interest on deposits	11.4	4.0	1.5	1.7	1.1	1.6	
Total investment income	**16.9**	**13.3**	**9.2**	**8.9**	**8.3**	**9.0**	
Total incoming resources	**100.0**	**100.0**	**100.0**	**100.0**	**100.0**	**100.0**	
Number of organisations with incoming resources	80,608	53,971	21,470	4,128	438	160,615	

Source: NCVO, GuideStar Data Services

(Income Definitions: Micro is less than £10,000; Small is £10,000 to £100,000; Medium is £100,000 to £1 million; Large is £1-10 million; and Major is over £10 million)

This table will help you to work out if your organisation's income profile is 'typical'. If it is not, there may be more income opportunities for you. At the time of going to press this is the latest available table. Figures will change only a little each year. Check the latest NCVO Civil Society Almanac.

How to use this table

Start by looking at the column that fits your organisation size (see the definitions in brackets immediately under the table). The figures in the columns are the percentages of all charity income in this size of organisation which come from the source listed in the first column.

So if for example, you have an income of less than £10,000 per year and if you are typical of organisations your size then you look at the first column of figures and see that 32.4% of your income will be donated by individuals and 30.4% earned from individuals. Only 6.1% will come from local or national government or the National Lottery as grants.

This table has three important uses here:

- it emphasises the wide variety of income markets in which we can choose to operate. If we are active in three or more income markets, then if one lets us down it is only a challenge and not a disaster.

- it indicates the size of each income source

- it shows how well or badly we are performing in comparison with other organisations of a similar income size. So to continue with the example of the organisation of under £10,000 per year: if you are raising 50% of your money from individual donations you are doing well compared to the average of 32.4%. But if you are only getting 5% from this source you are underperforming.

More information

A very practical and thorough way to explore the various income sources available and their use to you, is to use **NCVO's Sustainable Funding Project (SFP) website** – in particular their *Income Assessment Tool* – **which will help to** identify and assess the right income streams for you.

NCVO SFP's *Funder Needs Analysis* will help you to orientate the different approaches required for each type of funder.

Ansoff Matrix (adapted)

This is a handy conceptual framework which tells us how hard a new fundraising initiative is likely to be, and predicts its chances of success. Option 1 is the easiest to undertake and is most likely to be successful. Option 4 is the hardest and least likely to succeed. In my experience many charities ignore Option 1 (the best option) and are seduced by the excitement of Option 4 (the worst option). Grant-making trusts also tend to encourage applications that are in the higher risk segments.

Option 1: Expanding **existing** fundraising or earned income products in **existing** markets

In this scenario, the fundraiser or service promoter knows how to deliver the product efficiently and knows how the donors or consumers will react so the two biggest variables are very low risk (eg selling more raffle tickets by more people selling them over a longer time period, or by taking Talking Book memberships to more Local Authorities). Also this option can be very desirable in social policy terms. Many VCOs are proud to publicise their successful beneficiary services but they are much more secretive about what proportion of their target group is being helped. Often it is as low as 5% to 10%. So generating more income for an existing product might increase beneficiary market penetration up to 30% or 40% or more.

Option 2: Expanding **existing** fundraising or earned income products into **new** markets.

More risky because while you know what you are doing, you do not know the new kinds of donors/customers and how they are going to react (eg using an existing product, such as taking a terminally ill child to Disneyland, normally fundraised from individuals and offering it to a corporate potential donor).

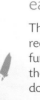

Option 3: Taking a **new** fundraising or earned income product to an **existing market**

Developing a new product takes time and experimentation to be successful and requires more investment in research and development (R&D) than Option 2 above. It requires R&D on the new service to the beneficiary and R&D on the associated funding product being taken to the funder (donor, trust, commissioner etc).

Option 4: Taking a **new** fundraised or earned income product to a **new** market.

This is most risky and costly in terms of time and money. It requires even more R&D (eg developing a service and fundraising product suitable for the corporate market where the organisation has little experience, knows few people and does not know how decisions are taken).

Conclusions

- Options 1 and 2 are most likely to succeed
- Options 1 and 2 are most likely to increase the number of beneficiaries accessing your service

A re-framing of the Ansoff Matrix can be found in the **NCVO SFP's New Product, New Market Tool**

Chapter 2: marketing analysis

SWOT – analysis of strengths, weaknesses, opportunities and threats

Before starting any new income development initiatives it is important to understand particularly your organisation's capacity or ability to undertake the new income generation work, both in terms of time and skills. For example, if no-one has any experience of working in or with commercial companies, it makes no sense to venture into corporate fundraising unless you have the money to invest in external professional advice. Conversely, if you have a good organiser with a lot of 'get up and go', who is prepared to organise a fete or raffle, then that is a good starting point. If they have done it before, even better – a real set of strengths.

There are many ways of doing an assessment of internal strengths and weaknesses but a straightforward way is to list strengths down the left hand side and weaknesses down the right, either alone or in a group. This will give you a good steer on what kinds of income development activities you and your colleagues have the time, knowledge and skills to undertake.

Another very practical tool to help you assess how financially sustainable your organisation might be is to use the **Sustainable Sun Needs-Analysis Tool** from **NCVO SFP**. It will help you see where you need to invest in new capacities.

Opportunities and threats refer to the external environment – outside your organisation. An opportunity might be:

- the availability of a refurbished community hall with kitchen facilities, which could open up a whole raft of possible fundraising events

- the arrival of a new enthusiastic head of a secondary school who might be more open to students being involved in fundraising activity

- the arrival of a recession resulting in many more vacant shops that might be used a charity shop

A threat might be:

- the arrival of a fundraiser from a national organisation working in the same area as you

- the arrival of a new secondary head who is not prepared to carry on fundraising for you with his/her students because it is not considered sufficiently 'educational'

Positioning

What is the positioning of your charity and what do you want it to be? You might want people to think your non-profit is modern and efficient but sensitive and caring. But if people actually think of it as rather brash and pushy, patronising, paying out too much on administration etc, then you need to know. You can employ market research agencies to survey people independently and anonymously or if you have no money, you can ask your friends to tell you what they imagine their friends think of your organisation.

What is the relevance of positioning to sustainable funding? You need to ensure that the methods you use do not inadvertently undermine your intended message. So if your fundraising appeal letter is too strongly worded with a (brash) hard sell that makes you feel pity towards beneficiaries and you get donors' names wrong, then you are directly contributing to your negative image. But this is not an argument for weak appeal letters – they can still be strong and not patronising, pitiful or brash. A method to reduce the likelihood of this is to run the draft past some of your beneficiaries. At RNIB I always asked for the feedback of a group of six blind people before I would sign off the copy of an appeal letter; and would ask for changes it they felt it was misrepresenting the position of blind and partially sighted people.

Competitor analysis

Competitor analysis is quite close to threat analysis and if you think you have covered it there, then leave this out. Certainly it is useful to delay using this tool until you are clear on what income raising activity you want to expand or launch. Then you can see more clearly what specific competition you are up against and just how damaging it might be.

For example, say if you have another cancer organisation working near you, this looks like severe competition. But if they focus on sponsored event fundraising and you are planning to open a shop, and, further, they are a children's cancer organisation and you focus on adults – then the competition will be unproblematic. But if they already have a shop, even though your focus is on adults, you would probably be ill advised to open a second, unless you have no other attractive fundraising options available.

So the competition that could scupper your income generation can come from an apparently duplicate cause (cancer) or a duplicate method (shops). Not spotting duplicate method competition is where many charities come unstuck. Who else holds bingo sessions, where and when? Who else has a fundraising dinner, where and when?

For national charities competitor analysis is less about damage limitation and more about keeping an eye open for up and coming income generation ideas and methods. For example the smart charity spots the early entry of a new funding method, monitors progress, learns, and piles in hard after a few months of lessons learned. This happened with 'one to one' street fundraising (chugging), 'buy a goat' at Christmas, national telephone raffles and overseas sponsored holiday challenges.

Chapter 2: marketing analysis

Intuitive thinking

At this point, you have a lot of information, but none of it on its own will tell you what to do. This is what you should have:

- Ansoff advising you about expansion using new products and/or new markets.

- market analysis, which allows you to compare your income profile with the total market income profile for organisations of your size and tells you which income sources to consider.

- some idea of your organisation's capacity to adopt different fundraising methods (strengths and weaknesses).

- a rough and ready knowledge of the range of income generation methods available (and if you haven't, see Stage 2, below).

- a good idea of what your competitors are doing and whether you can compete head to head or prefer to do something different.

- an understanding of how you want people to think of your organisation, which may well help you to choose between different options as some may be unacceptable (eg cold telephone calling).

So now it is time to do some hard thinking in the light of your marketing analysis so far. You need to draw up a few income generation methods that can be expanded or launched for the first time (say between three and six). You can then apply some marketing principles and tools to this shortlist.

Segmentation

Segmentation is the most important tool in marketing. It is generally accepted that mass produced approaches to income generation don't work (eg Dear Sir/Madam). We also know that personalisation, where we really get inside the head of our contact and produce proposals around their specific requirements (needs) and interests (wishes), works best. Segmentation is a way of combining the efficiency of mass production with some of the advantages of personalisation. You can achieve this through grouping people/organisations with similar needs and wishes into segments. This means that most of the preparation work will be common to everyone in the segment – mini mass production. So for example in the Gift Economy sector, a promising segment (a target segment) might be females over 50 who attend places of worship. That allows you to draft an ask that will appeal widely across this group. It also provides you with a way of reaching them, ie through places of worship and the religious organisations that run them. (In marketing, this is sometimes called a distribution channel). An example from the structured market might be all the officials in the NHS responsible for third sector commissioning. So to be useful, target segments have to be:

- people or functions that have common needs and wishes relevant to what we are 'selling' to them

- be reachable in some practical way

'Segmentation = pragmatic: group people together who will respond to similar messages'

Stage 2: Helping you to choose which income generation method to use

Voluntary income including the gift economy and grant funding

Categorising fundraising methods is problematic. Some of the most logical lead to repetition – for example by market or by size or type of VCO/charity. The way I tend to do it is **by fundraising method, ordered in a rough and ready way by increasing cost ratio.**

So in the list that follows, methods coming first will tend to be more cost effective than methods coming later – but there are always exceptions depending on the skills and knowledge contained within your organisation and its people.

'Cost ratio = how much you are likely to get back for your investment. So if you have a cost ratio of 20%, for every £1 you invest (in staff time or resources), you should see £5 in return. However, a cost ratio of 50% would only achieve £2 for every £1 invested'

Chapter 2: which income method?

This is the last Will and Testament

Legacies

Are legacies a realistic aspiration?

I find people often dismiss legacies as a method and this can be through ignorance. Here are some of the arguments I hear:

- 'legacies take too long to materialise' – actually most bequests are realised between two and four years after a person makes their last will

- 'very few people make charitable bequests' – approximately 10% of wills include charitable bequests

- 'people don't like us to talk about wills and death, and it will scare off our existing donors' – most older people think about their future quite regularly and thinking about whether they need to update their will is part of that

- 'changing your will is a complicated and expensive undertaking' – not really, solicitors have become more competitive recently. There are three kinds of charitable bequests: pecuniary, residuary and specific. **Pecuniary** is where you leave a specified amount (say £1,000) to someone or some organisation and it is easy to execute through a simple codicil added to your will (a codicil is like a legal 'PS' on the end of the will). A **residuary** legacy – the remainder (or part of the remainder) of the value of the estate – is more complicated to execute but tends to be much more valuable for the recipient VCO. A **specific** bequest is normally an item – eg jewellery, or land.

It is true that under normal circumstances we are talking years rather than months. But devoting time to legacy promotion will transform your organisation in due course and could be the single biggest income generation intervention you make, providing incredibly useful untied development money.

How do you achieve legacies?

From being the fundraising Cinderella, legacy marketing has become a serious business, producing excellent results. Large charities have done particularly well but there is no reason why smaller, local VCOs cannot cash in on this highly cost effective method:

- make your need known, probably through 'add on' messages in your other communications to donors

- emphasise how easy it is to add a codicil to an existing will specifying a particular amount and offer a draft codicil

- encourage people to let you know they have added a codicil and offer a pledge form that they can fill in, which you can acknowledge

- if you are a national organisation with sufficient money, consider employing a legacy officer. If you are a local one and cash strapped, try and interest a local will-making solicitor to give pro bono support. They may be more interested than you think because it may bring them new clients for the other services they offer. If there is a competitive advantage problem, get a pro bono offering from more than one local solicitors group.

Useful further reading

- The NCVO introductory guide to legacy fundraising

- Charity legacy code of conduct at the Institute of Fundraising

- Legacy Foresight – analysis and forecasts about legacies

- Join the Legacy Marketing Yahoo group

- Creating a lasting legacy, article from Charity Times

- knowhownonprofit.org has a legacy section

Take a look at the NCVO website for an introduction to another related method – in-memoriam giving

Links available from
www.ncvo-vol.org.uk/ arm/resources

Trusts and foundations

This is another highly cost effective income generation method which should be delivering a cost ratio of between 5% and 15%. This is how you should develop your strategy:

- find out which trusts are active in your cause area and/or geographic area if you are a local VCO. This is easily done by examining the annual reports of other VCOs in your cause area/geographic area (especially if you operate at the local level)

- study their grant guidelines if they have any, to see what the trust wants to/is prepared to fund; and exactly how they want applications made

- check the names of the trust committee members and any advisers they may use to see if anyone in your VCO knows any of them. See how any informal contact can be subtly engineered, but be careful not to appear to be lobbying – more on the lines of 'do you have any advice'

- use any legitimate, sensible reason to seek advice from the trust secretary/grants officer on which areas of your work the trust may be interested in. This achieves two things. First, it gets you noticed, so when your application comes in it may be recognised. Second, you will have received advice on which part or angle of your work is more likely to fit in with the trust's priorities/preferences

'Grants databases are getting increasingly sophisticated – Funding Central is updated daily and allows you to tailor your search to your organisation's profile and create a shortlist of relevant trusts and foundations to apply to. However, a successful fundraiser will never rely on just one source of information – visit the funder's website, find out who they've funded previously, speak to them if possible and gain as much information about what type of applications they would like before you apply'.

Graham Collins, SFP Programme Manager

Useful links

Making applications

- Funding Central will sign post you to advice, plus interactive tools to assess how you're doing.

- Directory of Social Change (DSC) publishes a number of grant-making directories. Look at their publication lists. They also offer grant-making database software accessible online. Their major publications are available in reference libraries and at your local Council for Voluntary Service.

- Research from DSC about the terms and conditions set by grant givers. Learn from their critical conditions research.

- Fit4funding is the website of the Charities Information Bureau who provide funding advice for community groups and voluntary organisations. They also have a monthly newsletter and a free grantfinder database.

- NCVO's page on trusts and foundations has information about making an application.

- knowhownonprofit.org has an excellent piece on trust fundraising

Finding out about sources of funding

- Funding Central – NCVO's free funding opportunities site will send you weekly funding alerts alongside their web-based search.

- Community Development Foundation – gives grants to community and voluntary groups working to improve communities.

- Grants guide from Welsh Assembly Government – for those based in Wales.

- Keep up to date with new grants by following grant givers or organisations that list new funds on Twitter. TweepML Funding has a useful list.

Links available from
www.ncvo-vol.org.uk/ arm/resources

Chapter 2: which income method?

Big gift/major donor fundraising

This is another highly cost effective method, which should be delivering a cost ratio of between 10% and 20%. It is not quite so good as trusts because the lead times between starting and succeeding are longer (between one and three years) and the time spent on supporting and engaging the major donor after receiving the gift is much greater (many major donors are a new generation of wealthy people and/or have large personalities and strong views).

What is a major gift? This depends on your organisation size. For a larger national organisation it is probably £100,000 and above. For a small local organisation it might be £500.

Major donor gifts have increased in the last few decades because of the growing number of significantly above average earners with high disposable incomes. Not all such people will give significant sums and the only way you can find this out is to get close to them. Giving can depend on their levels of confidence – their confidence in feeling they have made it and have more than enough to live on; their confidence that one way or another they will continue to make money (if you feel very precarious economically, however rich you are, you feel you need to keep lots of money in reserve).

> 'Try to ensure the potential donor feels attached to the organisation'

Relationship marketing

The aspect of marketing which you must use in recruiting and retaining major donors, is **relationship marketing**, covered in the section below. Using this approach will multiply your chances of continuing success. If you are trying to attract more than one major donor, you need to think how you can attract pre-formed groups of major donors. For example if quite a few wealthy people are members of the local golf club, this presents an opportunity. Attracting just one of their number as a major donor means:

- first, that person can be a helpful bridgehead into more club members

- second, when you are involving several of them in, say a social (bonding) event in your organisation, they will feel more comfortable at it because they will know other attendees.

If attaching yourself to a pre-formed social group is not viable, you need to build your own group. A traditional way of doing this is to persuade a much respected member of a group you are trying to engage, to **chair a committee** (typically a national or local dignitary, company chair or CEO, or celebrity). Provided you can make the committee meetings sufficiently interesting and entertaining, these meetings provide an excellent vehicle to achieve a variety of **bonding mechanisms**:

- social bonding (they like meeting and telling others they were with Sir Fred Bloggs the other evening)

- structural/administrative bonding (fix dates in advance, circulate agenda, minutes etc,)

- customised bonding (take pairs of committee members/ potential major donors on field visits and ask them to report back their experiences to the main committee).

The process

Quite a few major donor fundraisers subscribe to a number of steps that you need to go through to achieve a major gift, Jeff Shear[1] describes eight steps:

1 – Identify
This can be as straightforward as asking your trustees to name all the people they know who might be able to give £500

2 – Research
What can you find out about these people? What are their interests and passions. Who knows them?

3 – Plan
You may need to plan to have four names for every one gift. Who is going to try and interest them, who is going to ask, when?

4 – Involve
How are you going to do this? Take them on a visit or invite them to a meeting or reception or some other social event. Take them to lunch. Who does this can be important – some donors want to meet the workers, others want to meet the important people like your President.

5 – Ask
This is the part that most VCOs find really difficult. Here are Jeff Shear's tips:

- if you can get away with it, never mention money at the ask, instead ask them to get involved and pledge their support

- tell them about what their gift could achieve

- know when to shut up. You will be far more nervous than they are and you will be tempted to start babbling and never stop.

- be prepared to answer lots of questions, so prepare well

- it will be a big decision for them and they may well want to go away and talk to their family and accountant

- you don't have to close the deal – the challenge is not to get a no

- rehearse your pitch.

6 – Close
Even if you have a yes, you need to agree on exactly when and how they will pay – will it be a cheque or card? Will the VCO be able to claim Gift Aid or will it come via a charity account on which gift aid is already claimed?

7 – Thank
I have covered this above. But in summary this must be immediate, written as well as oral, genuine, fulsome, and non-formulaic.

8 – Stewardship
This is maintaining the relationship during the donation period. It's no good ignoring a donor for three years and assuming they will still be interested. They need visits, progress reports invitations to events etc – with easy room for them to say no.

[1] www.knowhownonprofit.org

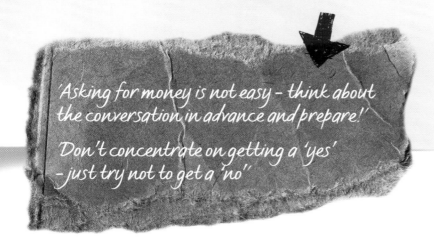

'Asking for money is not easy – think about the conversation in advance and prepare!'

'Don't concentrate on getting a 'yes' – just try not to get a 'no''

Links available from
www.ncvo-vol.org.uk/arm/resources

Useful links

- The NCVO introduction to Major Donor fundraising

- Best practice for major donors fundraising (Institute of Fundraising)

- Who is your next major donor? (Philanthropy UK)

- 'Why rich people give' book (Philanthropy UK)

- Carnegie's hymn to wealth

- The Big Give website helps charities promote projects they are seeking funding for. From small to significant amounts, the site is well used by donors.

- Charity Base connects you with individual and corporate donors in the UK.

Chapter 2: which income method?

Corporate giving

Corporate giving is a popular but often unsuccessful way of building income. This is because companies in the UK do not give a large proportion of their income and only 3% to 5% of charity income comes from this source.

This income strand has two streams, the straight **corporate donation** (reasonable cost ratio of 20%) because they are relatively uncomplicated, consisting of money and/or gifts in kind with application procedures more akin to trusts; and **corporate sponsorship** where the income package can be substantial but the demands on you are high, often backed up with a service level agreement specifying, for example how many more customers the company needs to recruit through the deal for it to be renewed for a second year; or specifying what kind of sales uplift the deal has created. Consequently the cost ratio is higher, as much as 30 to 40%.

Some people would dispute this but I believe it is important to cost in all the extra time spent, for example by VCO service delivery staff in fulfilling the corporate service agreements.

All the traditional tools of marketing are useful here especially **segmenting and targeting.**

For example:

- as a national disability charity, are there companies who have a financial/trade interest in your cause area (but watch out for unintended, apparent endorsement)?

- for example, as a local charity can you identify a segment of all companies with a turnover of between £1–£3 million that are within a five-mile radius and who are not part of a national chain?

How you get into the companies (distribution in the marketing mix) and how you sell in your cause can be tough. More companies are introducing 'beauty parades' where they get several charities to compete through bids and physical presentations to sell in your proposal.

Useful links

- NCVO's introduction to Corporate Fundraising

- Corporate Support (NCVO) – how to sell yourself

- www.knowhownonprofit.org

- Fundraising through partnerships with companies (Charity Commission) – this covers issues such as

- Helping companies helping charities (CAF) – research survey report into corporate giving.

'Only 3–5% of charity income in UK comes from corporates!'

'We're coming to the marketing mix in stage three'

Events fundraising

This can range from the special event such as a film premiere, or race day through to a regular event such as a sponsored swim or walk. The more unusual and infrequent the event, the higher the risk. So events cost ratios in my experience can range from 20% to actually making a loss.

There is one top tip: concentrate as much planning, time and effort on recruiting attendees as you do on designing and implementing the event.

Nearly every event I have attended or helped organise could have benefited from more effort on recruiting attendees. Indeed one enormously embarrassing evening event I helped organise actually had more celebrities and staff than it had donors and potential donors.

But the marketing theory and tools are perfect for ensuring a successful event – especially the marketing mix of product, price, promotion, place, people, physical evidence, processes and philosophy:

- product – make sure you explore a suite of associated products, eg not just a dinner or social with a ticket price, but also a raffle of £5 or £20 notes, an auction using donated items, and a collecting bucket at the end. Also make sure that your cause is featured in a pro-active way

- price – how much do you charge? But also look out for the hidden 'psychological' prices eg having the event clashing with the final of the X Factor

- promotion – how are you going to advertise/promote (posters, editorial, adverts in advance)? – who is going to sell tickets and how?

- place – can you find an attractive, affordable venue?

- people – two meanings here. First, have you got the right people to organise it (skills and experience)? Second, have you got a clear view of which groups you are aiming at and is there any likelihood of them clashing? For example, if you are mixing young and old is it an event where it won't matter, indeed might help (eg whole family can come)? Or will it mean neither group will like it (for example, a clash over music style)?

- physical evidence – attendees are strongly affected by physical signs. So shoddy promotional material or choosing a crumbling old hotel (even if it is cheaper) will predispose people into thinking the event will be poor.

- processes – especially around collecting the money – are important to design and test beforehand. With auctions, people (perhaps a little tipsy) bid generously and may baulk at paying in the cold light of next day, so have a credit card machine at the event. Sponsored runners and swimmers sometimes claim they have more sponsorship than they do and/or have difficulty getting their sponsors to pay up – so have rules and tips/advice.

- philosophy – make sure the activities around the event do not undermine your organisation's philosophy, especially towards beneficiaries. For example, if you are arguing that beneficiaries should not be patronised, make sure you choose images that reflect this.

Links for this section are available from **www.ncvo-vol.org.uk/arm/resources**

Chapter 2: which income method?

Links for this section are available from
www.ncvo-vol.org.uk/ arm/resources

Local fundraising

Local fundraising is hugely important to local VCOs as greater volunteer involvement means they can have lower cost ratios than can be achieved by a national organisation. The large nationals can have ratios up to 50-75%. They justify this because an active local profile brings increased levels of awareness, which in turn is assumed to increase legacy income.

All the methods of fundraising we have covered so far can be used locally or nationally, but there are many more. Some of the methods include:

- street collections
- raffles
- shop counter collection
- sponsorship
- buying goods from a charity
- appeal letters
- attending a charity event
- standing order/direct
- door to door collection
- buying in a charity shop
- church collection
- collection at work
- pub collections
- jumble sale purchases
- subscription/membership
- payroll deduction

Below are some figures from NCVO's UK Giving publications. Unfortunately we don't have any up to date figures for the individual fundraising methods, but the figures below help you to gain an idea of what is important and how this has been changing over time.

% of donors

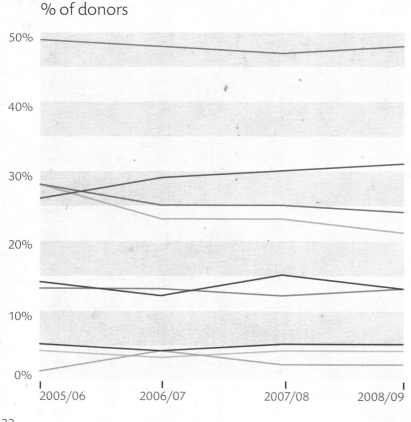

50%
40%
30%
20%
10%
0%

2005/06   2006/07   2007/08   2008/09

% of amount given

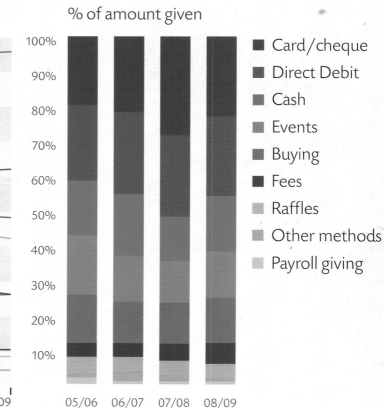

100%
90%
80%
70%
60%
50%
40%
30%
20%
10%

05/06   06/07   07/08   08/09

- Card/cheque
- Direct Debit
- Cash
- Events
- Buying
- Fees
- Raffles
- Other methods
- Payroll giving

Direct marketing (direct mail)

Direct mail, sometimes called appeal letters, has long been the dominant form of direct marketing but this has changed as the distribution channels to the public have changed. So in the early 1970s press adverts were used to attract donations. As address lists of potential donors became commercially available it was direct mail; now digital channels are rapidly rising in importance (eg email to desktops, messaging to handheld computer devices). We tend to think of direct marketing as a national activity but they can and should be applied by local VCOs.

The most common distribution channels for direct (ask) marketing are:

- TV and radio (local as well as national)
- inserts into other organisations' mailings (including magazines)
- adverts, hopefully combined with editorial stories in any medium (press, radio, internet)
- appeal letters posted or delivered door to door
- telephone
- face to face asks in the street
- email
- texting.

The best direct marketing campaigns may well use a mix of these methods. And remember all these methods can be used locally (except TV).

The marketing principles remain the same whatever the method or channel. It is essential to cover all aspects of the charity marketing mix (product, price, promotion, place, people, physical evidence, processes and philosophy) but my top tips are:

- make a **strong appeal** (the product) emphasising results/**impact,** making them as tangible as possible

- aim it, if possible, at a **target** segment of your market (the public)

- think carefully about **price** (or the requested donation)

- make it **easy to donate** immediately or quickly.

With the rise of huge databases of names, the second point above is less necessary but remains desirable. It is becoming as easy and cheap to contact 100,000 people as it is to contact 10,000. This can lead to sloppy marketing because there is no immediate penalty for reaching the 5% of people to whom your message is targeted, and not being bothered by the fact it is also sent to the other 95%. But remember, you can be turning the other 95% against you by intruding with unconvincing messages – which over time can be a problem.

Useful links

- NCVO's introduction to Individual Giving.

- Direct marketing code of practice (Institute of Fundraising)

- 7 top tips for direct marketing (NCVO)

- www.knowhownonprofit.org has a section within the fundraising part of the portal, on Direct Marketing, written by Stephen Pidgeon, one of the country's top experts

Don't forget all the links quoted in this publication are available from **www.ncvo-vol.org.uk/ arm/resources**

Chapter 2: which income method?

Contracts and commissioning – the structured market

This is definitely earned income, moving us into the structured market of defined purchasers such as health or local authorities and sometimes other VCOs. There is always a contract that is effectively a service level agreement between the purchaser and the VCO provider, laying out the quantity and quality of service required under various circumstances; but also the price to be paid, how payment is passed over and on what time scale – often related to the units of service delivered.

Sales strategies

Contracts and commissioning is a growing segment of the income market, moving from 40% to 50% of the total VCO sector income between 2000 and 2007. How to deal with this rapid increase in state contracts has been a problem for our sector. Some VCOs like The Children's Society refused to embrace contracts in the early 1980s, whereas Action for Children did. While in the 1980s the two organisations were of similar size, Action is now much larger with a huge contract income.

However, the contracting/structured market income source is not new, it has been around for hundreds of years. What is new is the rate of growth since the Thatcher governments of the 1980s to the point that some people feel the sector's independence is being threatened. I think this argument is important but exaggerated. For example, MENCAP and Scope earn well over 50% of their income from different parts of government without their independence being threatened or their campaigns blunted. Why is this? Because they have many dozens of different commissioners who are independent of each other. There is a widely held view in commerce that a company should never allow any one purchaser/customer to provide more than 10% – 15% of its income. VCOs like MENCAP and Scope follow that rule and earn income from hundreds of independent local and health authorities. However if state bodies were to form purchasing consortia, that would be a real threat to our independence.

Local VCOs are in a real dilemma here. For some in the social care sector it is common for one local authority to provide well over 50% of a VCO's income. This does threaten independence of action. One solution is for borough-wide VCOs to combine into cross-borough bodies to the extent that any one local or health authority purchasing unit would never comprise more than one sixth (17%) of their income.

Some tools to help you secure contracted income:

The marketing framework is ideal for designing and modifying the contracted service from a VCO to a purchaser in ways that benefit the beneficiaries.

The marketing framework tool combines the charity marketing mix with the analytical tools of marketing research, segmentation, positioning and other player analysis and provides an ideal tool for designing or modifying a contracted service offering. It is included at the end of this publication.

In addition, the nonprofit customer focus tool provides a way of ensuring that all the parties to a service contract have their needs and wishes identified and considered. This is important because commissioned services will fail if the needs of all the customer groups are not met.

See **marketing framework** tool on **p44**
See **customer focus tool** on **p42**

Using the nonprofit customer focus tool with contracts and commissioning

Beneficiaries

This is the group of people who are the primary beneficiaries of the contracted service, for example the clients, students, patients or audience depending on whether the service is in social care, education, health or the arts. It is **their needs and wishes that must be paramount** and these can be elicited by three main methods

1) Market research among the beneficiaries themselves using quantitative (numerical) and qualitative (descriptive) methods

2) Representation of beneficiaries on the advisory and decision-making groups of the service

3) The views of front line service staff who often have the greatest depth of knowledge of the beneficiaries.

Funders

In this structured market the funders will have needs and wishes that will hopefully coincide with those of the beneficiaries, but they will nearly always have additional needs and wishes that cannot be ignored otherwise there will be no contract won. If there is a clash between their needs and wishes and those of the beneficiaries then the latter should dominate. Not only is this hierarchy justified morally, it is a legal requirement for registered charities to meet the needs of their beneficiaries in order to be registered and receive tax benefits. While all this may seem obvious, there are many instances where the bidding charity puts the needs and wishes of the funder/commissioner above those of the beneficiaries they were previously targeting – this can lead to mission drift.

Stakeholders

These are the people who have a real stake in the project (in addition to the other three groups). Normally these will be staff and volunteers in the delivery VCO, VCO trustees and possibly major supporters, formal beneficiary representatives etc. If you cannot meet the needs and wishes of this group things will come unstuck rapidly.

Regulators

It is amazing how often this group is forgotten. (Until they announce an inspection, or challenge one of your returns.). For example, contracting may require you to set up a separate company or charge VAT differently. A mistake on the latter can be costly.

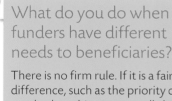

What do you do when funders have different needs to beneficiaries?

There is no firm rule. If it is a fairly small difference, such as the priority order of the needs, then this can normally be handled. Take a visiting service for older people for example; the older people may have a priority of reducing their loneliness, the local authority funder may be much less interested in that and much more concerned about maintaining their independence to reduce their chance of needing residential care. In fact focusing your service on combating loneliness is likely to keep people's confidence up and keep them independent for longer. So provided the relationships are managed, there is no major problem. But consider another example of an employment rehabilitation programme for newly disabled people; the government may only be prepared to fund employment elements such as computer skills. You know that before they will be able to learn and apply computer skills the newly disabled people need social rehabilitation to regain confidence and competence with daily living (eg how to cook with only one arm or no sight). However the Employment Service will not pay for this (despite your lobbying). So your choices are:

- to refuse the money because the service will not be effective and indeed demoralise the disabled person even further (they know how to use a computer but cannot live independently for want of daily living skills training)

- provide early social rehabilitation services out of VCO reserves and then use government money for the subsequent employment rehabilitation

- target your employment rehabilitation service on people who do not need social rehabilitation

Choice 1 at least stops you and the government making things worse. Choice 2 is costly to you but is effective for the beneficiary. Choice 3 is effective but may lead to mission drift away from those most in need towards those who are coping. The choice selected will be determined partly by your resource position and partly on your assessment of, say, the chances of persuading another government department responsible for health to pay for the social rehabilitation.

Chapter 2: which income method?

The practicalities of tendering and contracting

Richard Gutch describes top tips and common errors[2]

Top Tips

- ensure the service being delivered fits the aims and objectives of your organisation

- ensure the service is deliverable within the terms of the contract

- consider how delivering the service will affect your organisation's impartiality and ability to be an advocate for your beneficiaries. Will being reliant on income from a public body limit your ability to criticise its services?

- be sure that you understand how delivery will be judged

- apply full cost recovery rules to contracts – including the costs of preparing tenders

- check out the tax and VAT implications

- check employment law if new work involves taking on staff from another employer. Staff are often protected by TUPE – transfer of undertakings – rules that protect their jobs.

Common Errors

- missing the call to tender

- failing to express interest and therefore not receiving the documents

- failing to submit a pre-qualification questionnaire which debars you from the tender award phase of the process

- not providing the information required

- not answering the questions but providing information which can be regarded as 'marketing'

- basing the responses on unsupported assertions rather than evidenced claims

- not including the key documentation

- failing to adequately demonstrate effective management of risk

- missing submission deadlines.

[2]www.knowhownonprofit.org under the public service income section of funding and income

Links available from **www.ncvo-vol.org.uk/arm/resources**

Further sources of information

Richard Gutch's sections on www.knowhownonprofit.org give good compact guidance from a marketing perspective. Also see Procurement and Contracting to get a lot more detail.

www.ncvo-vol.org.uk/psd gives a good introduction to public service delivery as well as support for more advanced organisations.

There are a growing number of courses and consultancies offering help with bid writing, tendering and contract management. The following agencies can signpost you to these, as well as offering courses of their own:

- National Programme for Third Sector Commissioning

- NCVO Sustainable Funding Project (including the Public Service Delivery Network)

- NAVCA Commissioning and Procurement Unit

- ACEVO professional development events and courses

The open market – income/finance generation through trading, charity shops, social enterprise.

This section deals with the hard-edge end of earning money and profits by VCOs. This part of the market includes **unrelated trading for profit** directly to individuals, such as mail order gift catalogues and charity shops. Perhaps the ultimate in unrelated trading is the Christmas card market where thousands of charities compete with other charities and commercial card companies. Although these activities can increase awareness of the charity's brand they are unrelated (in the main) to the cause. Their primary task is to generate profits and awareness which can be invested subsequently into the cause. Marketing theory and tools are at their most transferable in this part of the VCO funding market, ie transferable from the commercial world to the charity world. This is because charities are often selling straightforward consumer goods (eg Christmas cards), competing in a market place where supply outstrips demand (whereas with beneficiary services it is so often the other way round). In the open market charities have to woo too few customers – the very setting in which marketing theory and its tools were developed in the commercial world.

Not all trading is unrelated to the mission of the charity. Cause related trading, such as the marketing of disability aids, does not have profit as its prime motivation – indeed this trading can often be loss-making. In this example, the cause is the *product* – making disability aids available. Some social enterprises are cause-related around the *process*, particularly through employing beneficiaries in the production and/or selling stages eg *Big Issue* magazine employing homeless people as sales reps; or recycling enterprises employing long term unemployed young/homeless people.

Marketing theory and tools are extremely helpful in ensuring that the charity products operating in the open market and aimed at individuals, are:

- what their customers want
- at a price they will pay
- communicated to them in an easy way
- delivered to them conveniently

and where they are services:

- delivered by competent people
- with tangible signs of quality
- and processes (such as booking) that are customer friendly.

In other words our old friend the (service) marketing mix.

All the analytical tools of marketing come into their own in the world of charity trading, social enterprise and shops:

- market research among customers (qualitative and quantitative)
- segmentation of the purchasers
- analysis of what your competitors are doing so you can learn from them
- finding out what your customers really think of your product so that your products can be improved and your promotion of them can be more realistic.

To find out more about the detail of **trading** go to Jim Brown's excellent guide on the trading section of the NCVO website.

To learn more about operating **shops** go to John Tough's book Setting Up and Running Charity Shops (The Association of Charity Shops). Also look at the section in www.knowhownonprofit.org on trading and go to the Association of Charity Shops

- Association of Charity Shops
- How charities may lawfully trade (Charity Commission)
- The Good Guide to Trading (NCVO)
- Trading (Finance Hub)
- eBay for Charity

Chapter 2

Stage 3: making your fundraising methods effective (Product development and maintenance)

So now that you have a shortlist of methods (stage 2) we can go into the specifics. Marketing theory helps us do that through the marketing mix. This tool was developed by Borden in the 1960s for FMCG – fast moving consumer goods such as soap, confectionery and drinks. It was expanded by Booms and Bitner in the 1980s to work with services. This is the version that I have found works best for VCOs, with one exception; I have added an extra element, philosophy, to ensure that organisational values are dominant in the marketing mix.

'A fundraising product is an idea that is shaped for the funder'

So the non-profit marketing mix in summary is:

1. Product (what are you 'selling'?)
2. Philosophy (what are your values?)
3. Price (how much are you asking for?)
4. Promotion (how will you advertise it, sell it etc.?)
5. Place (how will you distribute the income generation product?)
6. People (what kinds and numbers of people do you need to run the funding method?)
7. Physical evidence (to make what you are proposing more believable)
8. Processes (how can you make your product easy to take up, use and pay for)

The marketing mix

1. Product – designing the ask

Some people make the mistake of thinking that the service and its benefits delivered to the beneficiary (eg a visiting service for older people) is the same product and benefits being sold to the person/people who are providing the money (eg the recipient of a direct mail appeal letter or a Local Authority commissioner). It is not. The product delivered to an older person is predominantly a service whereas the one delivered to the funder is predominantly an idea.

So those responsible for VCO income generation:

• take the beneficiary service product and reshape it into an idea product

• select which beneficiary benefits are most likely to appeal to the funder and feature them

• make it as tangible as possible.

(Bruce 1994, re-framed 2005)

This means that two service descriptions are needed, one for the beneficiary market and one for the supporter (income provider) market. The one aimed at the funder is normally called the 'case for support' (but the two must be compatible).

So how do you *reshape* the service's benefits to maximise the appeal to the funder?

Examine the benefits the service provides to the beneficiary and select those most likely to appeal to the funder. For instance, in the case of a visiting service, it is designed to prevent isolation (loneliness) and maintain independence – giving the older person someone on whom they can rely. If the prospective funder is a commissioner, they are likely to find the maintenance of independence more convincing a reason to contract for the service because it saves the state money. If the funder is the recipient of an appeal letter, s/he is likely to find relieving loneliness more compelling because it is an emotional appeal.

What is not legitimate, however, is to choose a funder benefit that does not feature in the offering to the beneficiary. Some income generators in the disability and overseas development fields have in the past done just that. This is not only immoral but also damaging when it is exposed. The adverts in question invited potential donors to feel pity through showing pathetic, dependent images of the beneficiaries when the service product was designed to promote independence.

How and why do we need to make the income generating product tangible?

In the minds of the funder, whether they are a member of the public, trust official or commissioner, the service product is largely an idea and almost never a first-hand experience to them.

They will seldom, if ever, experience it as a beneficiary would. Consequently the income generator has to make the idea product as convincing as possible. So appeal letters are often quite detailed, describing exactly which tools or technical aids are being used and how much they cost; pictures of the service in action are used.

Often testimonials from satisfied beneficiaries can be effective – any legitimate evidence that can bring the proposition to life. For trust applications or contract bids, it can be very convincing and tangible to take willing beneficiaries along to a meeting – they can attest to the vital help they have received in their own way.

Chapter 2: making your methods effective

2. Philosophy – ensuring that the values of the organisation towards beneficiaries are evident in the ask

It is fundamentally important that the organisation's philosophy is included in the design of each beneficiary service. For example, if an organisation has a philosophy of empowering beneficiaries (maximising independence and self-growth and accepting some risk) then that needs to go into every service. An empowerment philosophy is quite different from a care philosophy (maximising safety and comfort, minimising risk, accepting high levels of dependency).

When designing the ask (the income generating product) it is critical that a beneficiary philosophy is built into the design (this was not the case with some disability and overseas development charities mentioned above).

It is even better if the philosophy is evident in the ask:

- first, the philosophy of the organisation is often central to the message it is putting out to society (eg to change attitudes and behaviour towards your cause – be it climate change, AIDS, overseas development etc.). If you miss the opportunity to educate funders then you miss a trick.

- secondly, medium and large organisations often have an overt or smouldering rift between their fundraisers and their service providers. In my experience this is at heart about different philosophies. If those working with funders can show that they are promoting the organisational philosophy then this increases active cooperation between them and the beneficiary service providers – cooperation that is essential to maximising income.

3. Price – what are you going to 'charge' the funders whichever market they are from?

The price you charge to funders cannot be drawn out of thin air, because some funders/purchasers will ask you to justify them. They have to be based on hard, replicable facts. But they also have to be affordable and seen as reasonable. If you are providing a product (service) that the funder needs desperately and no-one else is competing with you, then within moral limits you can charge what they are prepared to pay (the market price).

But normally the most you can charge is costs plus a margin to cover overheads (make sure you understand Full Cost Recovery), plus a little more to cover future research and development. But sometimes even that produces a price that the funder is not prepared to pay.

So, often you have to break your product down into different sub-packages with a variety of costs attached eg, £15,000 will buy an installed and fully functioning well; but £5,000 will buy all the materials; or £25 will buy and deliver a roller barrel to enable someone to drag the water from the well several miles to home. With contracts and trading, offering price choices is sometimes not so easy. It is not quite 'take it or leave it', but quite close, because you should not be prepared to go below a certain price threshold due to the effect on quality.

4. Promotion – how you are going to let people know about your product and persuade them to buy it? (this includes PR, advertising, selling etc)

Promotion (PR and advertising), sometimes called marketing communications, are areas where VCOs often excel. We are proud of our work and want people to know about it so we start with the right mentality.

The most critical question here is:

• whom do we want to reach, and what do we want them to do?

This leads to

• what message do we want to get across and what is the best method to deliver it?

In the case of commissioning – the 'structured market' – you may be looking to reach senior staff and elected/appointed members. In this case adverts in the local papers will be no good because our target groups (except the elected members) are quite likely to live outside the area and won't read local papers. But they all need local support and credibility, and they are all professional at what they do. So inviting them to visit your services (which you are 'selling' to their organisation) will be of interest. Arranging for the local MP or the Lord Lieutenant to be there at the same time is worth doing and getting a junior government minister to join would be a real coup. This is just as good PR as coverage in the press, important as that is.

Formal advertising tends to be used mainly by large national VCOs and involves marketing planning and advertising agencies, which is not the primary thrust of this publication.

One of the most trusted and tested promotional formulae, especially for **selling** is AIDA – the process starts with getting the funders ATTENTION, then his/her INTEREST, then DESIRE and finally ACTION (ie to buy or donate). With a cold purchaser you will have to start at the beginning but with a longstanding donor/purchaser you should already have their attention and interest.

For example, if you are applying to a new grant-making trust then you will not automatically have their attention, let alone their interest. A phone call to, or better a meeting with, the grants officer – well tuned to what you have read about their grant guidelines, will get their attention to your application (ie they will spot it when it arrives and link it to you, and your call). Because your call was thoughtful and well tuned to the trust's needs your modified application will get their interest and possibly even their desire. This scenario translates easily into the commissioning setting. In the case of a trust or commissioner, getting action is easy because most will automatically consider applications/bids received.

However, in the open market and other settings where the donor or purchaser was not demanding the product, turning the desire into the action of a donation or purchase is often tricky. In charities many people, especially trustees, shy away from making the ask as they are too embarrassed. It is critical that you have people around with courage/thick skin who are prepared to ask for a donation/decision.

Getting a yes is aided greatly by making it easy and convivial. An ask of 'I am sure you give to many charities. It would make such a difference if you would add us to your list?' is much more likely to get a yes than 'Will you give us a donation?' Offering a facility to pay by credit card and enclosing a freepost envelope will more likely get positive action. A discretionary sale of a service to a statutory authority is more likely to be achieved if the commissioner knows that his/her boss is very pro your cause/organisation. In short:

• think your way into the mind of the purchaser/donor and think what you can do to make it easier for them to give/buy

• remember this needs planning because some of those conditions take time to achieve. Enclosing a freepost envelope is fairly easy (but often forgotten); however building a professional and empathetic relationship with senior people in the local/health authority takes time.

I have dwelt on selling because in my experience VCOs are loath to do this, feeling embarrassed or resistant in having to 'beg' or be 'pushy'. But in the current climate any VCO which has no people with a sales mentality will be in dangerous decline before long.

'No begging! Keep it natural and friendly'

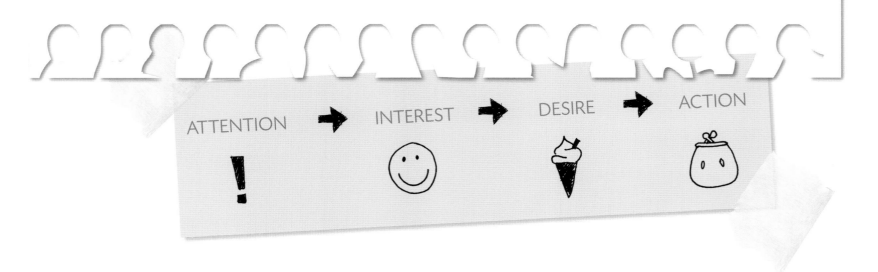

ATTENTION ➡ INTEREST ➡ DESIRE ➡ ACTION

Chapter 2: making your methods effective

5. Place – or how do you **distribute** the funding product or ask to the potential funder?

This marketing idea is particularly helpful for donations or sales (gift economy or open market) from the general public. More specifically, to maximise the cost effectiveness of your ask you might be aiming at upper socio-economic groups (A,B,C1, to use the marketing terminology), over 45 years old. What are your choices of place or distribution channel? Here are some ideas:

- fundraising or sales adverts in the newspapers (say the Daily Telegraph, Daily Mail, or local papers)

- joint editorial appeal for funds or sales with a newspaper (national or local)

- cold call telephone fundraising for donations or sales

- direct mail using purchased address lists of A, B, C1 people (better off); or volunteer delivered letters in middle class areas (if you are a local charity looking for sales or donations)

- a presence at events that would appeal to this target group, such as theatre evenings or concerts

- asking organisations and companies who also target this group to support your appeal, eg with a mention in a newsletter or by displaying your materials.

Your audience is roughly the same in each case as is your ask, but the method of delivering it is vastly different. The choice will be determined initially by:

- what you have successful experience of (use the Ansoff matrix discussed earlier)

- how the method fits with the brand image you are promoting

- what skills you have with the alternative distribution methods

- trial and error.

However, for grant funding there is normally only one option for distribution and that is highly prescribed by the grantor or commissioner (structured market) eg a required and highly structured text submission by a due date.

6. People – those who create and deliver the ask need to be able, trained and empowered

Enabling and controlling quality in income generation is very important and this requires well trained staff and volunteers. With products that are physical goods, they can be inspected before sale and dud ones removed and repaired for later sale. With idea and service products that is more difficult as often production and consumption happen at the same moment.

Thinking back to our explanation of the product above, most income generation activities are an idea, based on the description and demonstration of services. Both the product and the services are hugely dependent on the commitment and competence of the people running them. Any problems have to be rectified on the spot. This scenario requires well trained staff and volunteers with significant amounts of delegated discretion.

For example, if you are a major gift fundraiser charged with selling one particular product but it is going badly because the potential donor is no longer interested in the product in question, if it has not been planned beforehand, the fundraiser will have no discretion to introduce alternatives. Result – the rich donor is disengaged/lost.

'Fundraisers need flexibility and permission to use their discretion'

'how often and how quickly do you communicate with funders?'

8. Processes – very important but often forgotten, processes are particularly important in enabling payment and maintaining contact and appreciation

Apparently silly things make funders in all categories really annoyed such as:

- not being given the details of who the cheque or bank transfer is payable to.

- not issuing a receipt and/or not thanking at all (or not in a meaningful way)

- not following funder reporting requirements to the letter without gaining permission for a variation

- not keeping in touch on a regular basis (what is really bad is no contact until you want more money/to renew the contract/or to sell another product)

- not giving the funder significant public acknowledgement either because you did not realise they wanted it or you just haven't bothered to think about it (the ultimate is to omit reference to one funder in a setting where another is mentioned eg AGM, Annual Report).

Processes leads us neatly in to another section of marketing theory and practice that can make a huge difference to making our funding sustainable – relationship marketing.

Meaningful thank-yous!

Follow instructions

Public acknowledgement

Keep in touch

7. Physical evidence – evidence of your product needs to be carefully constructed, powerful and convincing

Remember your funding product may be very real to you but it is largely an idea product to the funder and so quite abstract/unconvincing. To make it more real to the funder you need powerful physical evidence to convince. We ascribe too much power to the spoken and written word. 'One picture is worth a thousand words' remains true.

My experience of taking along a satisfied beneficiary to speak is that it increases one's chances of a successful outcome by two or three times. The funder, whether they are a major donor, grantor, commissioner or purchaser, shows a huge leap in concentration and interest the minute the beneficiary is introduced.

There are many other forms of physical evidence such as:

- taking the potential funder to see the service to be funded at first hand

- the fundraiser having first-hand/personal experience of the issue

- model constructions and or architects drawings of the residential home, school, hostel one wants to build

- personal statements from satisfied beneficiaries; and where appropriate involving beneficiaries in the appeal

- photographs or even better, videos

- organisation charts, used appropriately, can help

Chapter 2: making your methods effective

Relationship marketing

– building a lasting relationship with our funders in order to maximise their loyalty and increase the chances that they will repeat their support over and over again.

What is relationship marketing and how does it help us?

Relationship marketing has much to teach us about achieving sustainable funding. It is a complex area and I am only going to pull out those concepts and tools that I have found really useful. Groonroos [3] one of the fathers of relationship marketing defines it as:

'... identifying and establishing, maintaining, enhancing and where necessary, terminating relationships with customers and other stakeholders, at a profit, so that the objectives of all parties are met, where this is done by mutual giving and fulfilment of promises.'

At its simplest we are trying to establish a **long term relationship** with our funders, whatever market they come from ie whether they are donors, grantors, commissioners or purchasers. This:

• builds two-way loyalty

• reduces some of the uncertainties of future funding

• avoids the much higher costs of finding new funders (it is argued that it costs five to ten times more to find a new customer/funder than to retain an existing one).

Some of the most important conditions we have to achieve to ensure a long term relationship are trust, commitment, cooperation and mutual benefit. So how do we do this?

[3]Groonroos, C. (1997) 'Value-driven Relational Marketing: From Products to Resources and Competencies', *Journal of Marketing Management*, 13, 407-4

'It costs 5-10 times more to find a new customer/funder than to retain an existing one'

How do we use relationship marketing to achieve strong long term relations?

The main ways are through:

• studying our funders closely to identify their characteristics, needs and wishes. This applies whether it is one major donor or commissioner, or 50,000 appeal letter donors or 50,000 mail order Christmas card purchasers. Only the data collection methods differ, not the aim. In the former case we will be using one to one interview and meetings, in the latter market research among a sample of customers will be more appropriate.

• spotting problems. In my experience VCOs are often too busy finding new funders rather than spotting problems in keeping existing funders happy. The first time some problems emerge is when repeat funding is sought – and this can be too late, the funder has already mentally disengaged.

• encouraging funders to say when they are really not happy.... We are really bad at this. Most VCO people, myself included, do not like to encourage complaints in any meaningful way. This view is a mistake. BA (British Airways) found they retained a far higher percentage of customers who complained (and had their problem dealt with) than among dissatisfied customers who quietly sat and fumed in anger.

'Well dealt with complaints = positive outcome!'

• ...and making superhuman efforts to put things right. This is not only important in its own right, it has immense benefits to help ensure sustainable funding. Service marketers have found that complaining customers who have their complaints resolved well, become more loyal than average, satisfied customers.

• appreciation. This is also immensely important. Lack of attention to this and the next header of recognition lead to more funder dissatisfaction than more or less anything else. Appreciation is at heart about saying thank you. Meaningfully and regularly. If the thanks aren't, and don't come across as, heartfelt and sincere they will backfire. Make your thanks specific to the setting and personal to the individual – for example: 'thank you for engaging so positively with the staff on your visit to the project you are funding – it gave them great encouragement.' Not 'thank you for sparing the time to visit the project you are funding. It was most appreciated'.

• recognition. Many funders will protest, often genuinely that they do not want any personal or organisational recognition. However, there is nearly always some way of giving a funder genuine pleasure through appropriate recognition – ranging from private acknowledgement in a three-way conversation between you, the funder and your President through to an acknowledgement on your website home page, annual report, AGM etc

What analytical tools and relationship strategies can marketing give us?

Below are the main strategies that can inform your methods and activities. For example an AGM with a good social event could implement all the bonding strategies below.

- **social bonding.** Here you provide settings in which your funders feel at home, enjoy themselves, feel part of the cause effort, and make or enhance links with other people they want to meet (often other funders)

- **structural bonding.** Here you involve funders in the formal or informal governance of the VCO as a whole or the part which they are funding, with options such as membership, participation in advisory groups, appointment to honorary positions (eg Vice President)

- **financial bonding.** Set up formal and informal agreements over payment of support over two or more years and other methods of tying in the funder to the organisation

- **customisation.** This encapsulates all the work achieved under the previous sections whereby the income generation product has been designed with the funder in mind (but with the beneficiary needs paramount).

'giving should be a positive experience, don't treat supporters and donors like a number'

All of the above ideas about relationship marketing will help keep your funders loyal. This has many benefits, but primarily:

- it helps to encourage repeat funding ie a sustainable income

- it reduces uncertainty

- and it reduces income generation costs because it is so much cheaper to keep an existing funder than to have to find a new one.

Chapter 3

Marketing helps sustainable funding

Case study of the Ariel Trust

The Ariel Trust is a service delivery charity in Liverpool helping young unemployed people to train and get into work.

- It received major funding from the EU, dependent on the North West's high deprivation status under EU rules

- It placed most of its trainees into an expanding network of local radio stations.

Then disaster crept up on them:

- The North West lost its preferential EU funding status and that major source of money began to dry up rapidly

- The expansion of local radio slowed to a halt.

This case study looks at how they used marketing theory and practice to re-orient, survive and thrive. It draws much of its material from the Ariel website and from discussion with **Paul Ainsworth, CEO of Ariel**, including our co-presented workshop to the NCVO Sustainable Funding Annual Gathering (June 09).

All about the Ariel Trust

Up until 2005/6 – expanding local radio and EU money – 'The Golden Age'

The Ariel Trust was founded in 1981 to open up the world of radio broadcasting to young people.

The catalysts for this ground-breaking venture were two studies, one by the British Broadcasting Corporation and the Independent Broadcasting Authority, the other by a leading charity, the Calouste Gulbenkian Foundation. These seminal reports both concluded that, although young people listened to a lot of radio, they had little understanding of how programmes were made and broadcast. Something needed to be done.

The result was the Ariel Trust, an independent charity, committed to bringing radio broadcasting and the opportunities that it has to offer within the reach of young people.

Ariel's original mission remains central: to develop communication skills, creativity and confidence through the medium of broadcasting; guide students to new achievements and open up access to new opportunities and jobs. In practice, many of these have been within the broadcasting industry, although they have never seen this as their primary goal.

Ariel has benefited from a growth in the radio industry in the North West from six stations in 1996 to 36 in 2006. The vast majority of these (85%) employed Ariel trainees and in two of the leading stations 10% of the staff began as Ariel trainees.

Ariel has never measured its success simply by the quantity of its broadcast material, but its productions do often feature on local and national radio, both BBC and commercial stations.

The vast increase in commercial radio stations in recent years is continuing to offer exciting new opportunities. Ariel continues to be in the forefront in working with this expanding sector. Training placements for Ariel students in the new commercial stations, and in BBC stations, have further strengthened their standing with the industry, evidenced by the numbers who have found jobs in local, regional and national radio stations.

Chapter 3: Case Study

How the Ariel Trust changed to sustain themselves; analysing the case study using marketing theory and marketing tools

Products (goods services and ideas)

In the middle noughties the North West lost EU Objective 1 status, which meant EU money dried up in a relatively short time. Secondly the radio industry started consolidating. This could have resulted in catastrophe – no money and no placements. But Ariel started by examining alternative markets and products (Ansoff Matrix) and decided on

• New products in existing markets

• New products in new markets.

What they did was to cut back on training young people for jobs exclusively in radio and develop new courses for the young people (**new products in existing markets**, a relatively safe option compared to **new products in new markets**).

As Paul, CEO says,

'We are particularly proud of a new apprenticeship programme. For over twenty years we have been training young adults for work in the radio industry. We are now training them to produce high quality education software for use in schools. This approach puts young people at the centre of this process; they create the ideas and develop the concepts'

(Paul Ainsworth, 2009, in his Big Lottery Review of the year).

So they have stayed with a market they know well and that is central to their mission (training young people) but have developed a different product (training in the production of educational software, rather than radio).

But what is clever and creative is that they are using this increasingly skilled work base of trainees to help produce **new products** (educational software packages) aimed at **new markets** (teenagers in schools). This is clever and creative because they have added value by producing a **product extension** – products arising out of the training courses, and **market extension** – by aiming at young people a few years younger than they used to work with. The dangers of market extension are reduced as the apprentice producers know the younger teenage group well – because they were that age a couple of years ago.

They are currently producing four educational programmes (**products**)

• **Plastered** looks at the consequences of binge drinking
• **Street Heat** focuses on anti-social behaviour
• **Senseless** empowers young people to challenge racism
• **Denial** explores the impacts of homophobic bullying

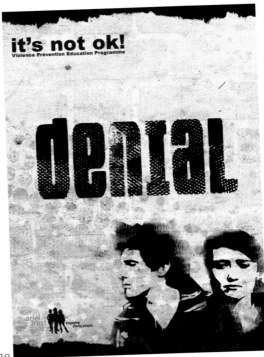

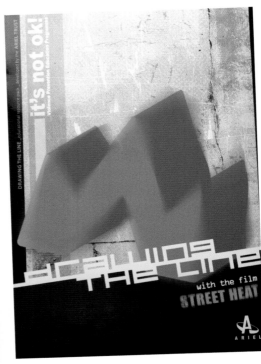

http://www.arieltrust.com/content/Services/ConsultancyServices.aspx

Google

E-Quote   Help

ariel trust

engaging
young people

Home   About Us   News   **Services**   Products   Downloads   Contact   APPLY

Pack Training & Consultancy

- **Developing New Packs**

Pack Training & Consultancy

Choose one of our packs and you can opt for additional training and support.

We offer:
- training to ensure you/ your staff make the most effective use of the packs
- support to develop operational partnerships
- support in the delivery of a pilot project
- evaluation and impact measurement
- support to roll out the resource across an area

We can advise you about useful applications, effective approaches, and help you to incorporate the resources into your work...with great success!

Note to L.E.A.'s:
We've developed a model that we believe represents the most effective approach to engaging schools, colleges or other agencies across an area.
We feel that operational partnerships (between teachers, youth workers, police officers, fire officers, and health professionals) give young people a clear message, and help to promote community cohesion.

For prices and further information, please get in touch.

Downloads

Consultancy: Building Partnerships (DOC, 160KB)

Street Heat pilot results (DOC, 53.5KB)

Plastered Evaluation Report (PDF, 486.69KB)

What is more they have used a mix of **marketing research, new product development and test marketing** to bring these products to market. This is illustrated in the following quote from the website:

'We have conducted and evaluated a number of pilot projects in the Merseyside area and have developed a model that we believe represents the most effective approach to using these resources and to engaging schools, colleges or other agencies across an area.'

But if the **teenagers are the end beneficiary customers** of these products, Ariel has to work through intermediary customers in order to reach the teenagers and have an impact. These **intermediary customers are teachers and heads of departments** in schools and colleges. Above is a website screen-shot of the sales promotion aimed at schools. It is selling the support service available to help them use Ariel's four products and the aims they are supporting.

'This type of operation partnership may be new to many and Ariel Trust can offer you support to develop local partnerships and roll out one of our education programmes across your local area.

The consultancy package can include:
- Support to develop operational partnerships
- Supporting the delivery of a pilot project
- Evaluation and impact measurement
- Support to roll out the resource across an area

A detailed description of the service and guide prices can be downloaded for the top of this page. If you would like to find out more please contact us to discuss your specific needs.'

Now compare the copy above with the copy overleaf. Both are aimed at teachers/heads of department in schools and colleges. Both are good but why is the promotion for Denial below, better?

These intermediaries' needs and wishes have to be met as well. The promotional material describes the position well except that it fails to emphasise 'what's in it' for the intermediary customers in relation to their primary purposes. This omission is corrected when the intermediaries receive promotional material specific to their group as in shown in the second quote overleaf aimed at teachers and schools in particular.

Chapter 3: Case Study

'DENIAL IS EVERY TEACHER'S DREAM

Rainhill High School's Head of English Steve Talbot cannot speak highly enough of Ariel's interactive learning resource 'Denial': "There's just so much in the pack, with so little for teachers to do".

'Denial', which focuses on bullying, homophobia, and peer pressure, was used by all of Rainhill High School's year 9 English classes over the course of a half-term.

As the lesson plans and worksheets cover a half-term of work, Steve suggested it is an "ideal transitional unit between Year 9 and 10".

The results at Rainhill High show why Steve talks so highly of this resource – 43 % of pupils achieved grades above those which had been predicted.

Rainhill High used the resource for both Key Stage 3 and 4, as the pack not only covers the new National Curriculum framework for Key Stage 3 but can also be used for pieces of GCSE coursework in Speaking and Listening and in Original Writing.

Indeed, Steve pointed out there are "a number of pupils in Year 9 who already have an A* piece of coursework before they go into Year 10".

He added:

"'Denial' is a win, win. It delivers effective citizenship education as well as significantly improving results in both Key Stage 3 and 4.'"

If you like puzzling things out, do NOT read the next paragraph yet, but form your own view as to why the second set of copy is more likely to appeal to teachers than the first.

You may form other views, but for me the key positive difference is that the second copy writer has put him/herself in the shoes of the intermediary customer (the teachers/heads of departments). S/he has thought through what is true about the project that is likely to appeal to the intermediaries. S/he has thought through what the teachers' needs and wishes are likely to be in the form of **benefits** to them in fulfilling their personal and organisational objectives. In other words its 'easy to use/takes very little work' (personal benefit to the teacher) and helps the students get better marks (organisational benefit, which may lead to personal benefit).

However, as I have said both promotions are good in other respects – they both follow **AIDA**

Attention – both grab attention right at the beginning with interesting copy, the first through the quirky product titles, the second through playing on the double meaning of denial

Interest – both gain the target market's interest by quickly explaining the relevance to teachers/heads of departments

Desire – here the second scores better. If I were a teacher with a challenging, possibly underperforming group of young people, I would really want this product

Action – this is fundamentally important. If people really want what you have, you need to make sure they can 'buy it' or signal their likely wish to buy it instantly and easily. Many sales are lost for want of this.

Also in terms of the marketing mix the Denial copy has something really tangible as physical evidence (the 6th paragraph) – the quote from a teacher with their name and school included, which gives the copy and its claims real credibility.

Other aspects of marketing theory ariel has used

Running through the marketing mix, product, promotion and physical evidence we have covered in the last section. That leaves price, place, people, processes and philosophy

Philosophy is the only piece of marketing theory that I have originated (Bruce 1994) and so, perhaps not unexpectedly, I think it is one of the most important, especially for VCOs. While much of what an organisation does can change in order to maintain financial sustainability, two things should not (except in the most extreme circumstances). The first is its primary beneficiary group and the second is its philosophy. Has Ariel had to change these in order to survive? The answer is 'No'. The **primary beneficiaries** remain young people, helped into work through the apprenticeship scheme, with a focus on communications, (originally radio, now educational software). Yes there has been some customer extension but this has cleverly been to an adjacent group, not school leavers but secondary school students. And the **philosophy** used in working with these young people has remained constant as is shown in its mission:

'to develop communication skills, creativity and confidence'

Price has been tackled, an element many charities seem unconfident on. The physical products and the services are priced at levels Ariel believes the market will pay. Earned income from goods and services has risen fast in the last three years and is coming close to replacing the hole left by the loss of EU funding.

Place or distribution has become a lot more complicated with the launch of the education software physical products and services. Ariel utilises a mix of on-line and on-site (schools and colleges) delivery methods.

People has been one of the most dramatic areas of change of the Mix for Ariel. To deliver a more marketing/sales orientated culture (moving from an almost exclusively social services one) has seen the rise of targets, the monitoring of performance, greater celebration of incremental improvements and a staff bonus scheme. As the Director Paul Ainsworth says, it can be caricatured in alternative ways:

• a stressful environment OR a modern organisation

• a bit like working in a call centre OR an entrepreneurial buzz

Processes – managing and serving customers has required major process change including the development of a customer data base, more streamlined invoice processing and extra reporting, particularly sales reporting against targets and billing.

So, has it worked?

So far it certainly has, which is a real accolade to staff and trustees given the elegance (but complexity) of the solution – product range extension and beneficiary customer extension. In practice this has meant new products into new markets which is the highest risk and most difficult of the four Ansoff options.

The next two or three years will be the decider. The new product categories and new intermediary and end target groups have been sorted. Now it is about delivery. What Ariel needs is to see the brilliant sales growth of the past two years continue and the maintenance of a multi-customer base (to prevent dependency). Of course there will be mediocre years, but a decided upward trend will reduce significantly Ariel's exposure to grant givers with their changing policies and priorities of grant aid in difficult times.

Chapter 4

Two charity marketing tools useful to ensure sustainable income

Customer focus tool

A simple way of defining marketing is **'meeting the needs of your customers within the objectives of your organisation'**. This begs the question **'Who are your Customers?'** The model that follows (Bruce 1994 and 2005) breaks customers down into four types and introduces the concept of **intermediary customers** ie the people who control access to your end customers and through whom you have to work. Your product has to be acceptable to all four of these groups.

Beneficiaries	Supporters	Stakeholders	Regulators
Clients	Donors	Staff	Charity commission
Students	Volunteer fundraisers	Representatives of beneficiaries	Local authorities (e.g. inspection of homes, schools)
Patients	Voluntary service workers	Committee members	Local community
Users	Advocates		
Purchasers	Purchasers		
Local public			
Members			
Audience			
Patrons			

Beneficiary Intermediaries	Supporter Intermediaries	Stakeholder Intermediaries	Regulator Intermediaries
Statutory providers	Religious leaders	Staff managers	MPs
Statutory purchasers	Company chief executives	Union representatives	Home Office
Commercial providers	School head teachers	Committee leaders	Local councils
Family purchasers			
Other voluntary organisation providers			
Policy-makers			
Decision-makers			

Chapter 4

Marketing framework tool

The **marketing framework** is a visual representation that shows how all the parts of the marketing process we have looked at above, fit together.

The first column lists all the main analytical tools to help you understand the relevant parts of the world out there. This can help you to create a successful product that will 'sell' well ie market segmentation, marketing research, other player analysis and positioning. You use these tools **to understand where, why and how your product is succeeding or failing.**

- the rectangle (second and third columns) entitled 'marketing mix' contains all the constituent parts of the product that you want your customers (donors, purchasers, commissioners) to 'buy'. You use these tools **to ensure all these different product parts are liked by your customers**

- the target market and take up behaviour are a description of the kinds of people you are aiming your Product at and the kinds of ways they behave in taking up or 'buying and paying' for your product (eg AIDA described earlier). These two parts of the framework **drive all the decisions on the marketing mix**

- Finally the broad arrow sweeping around the bottom indicates that when you have a decent volume of customers contributing sustainable income you **start again** and re-apply all the analytical tools in Column 1

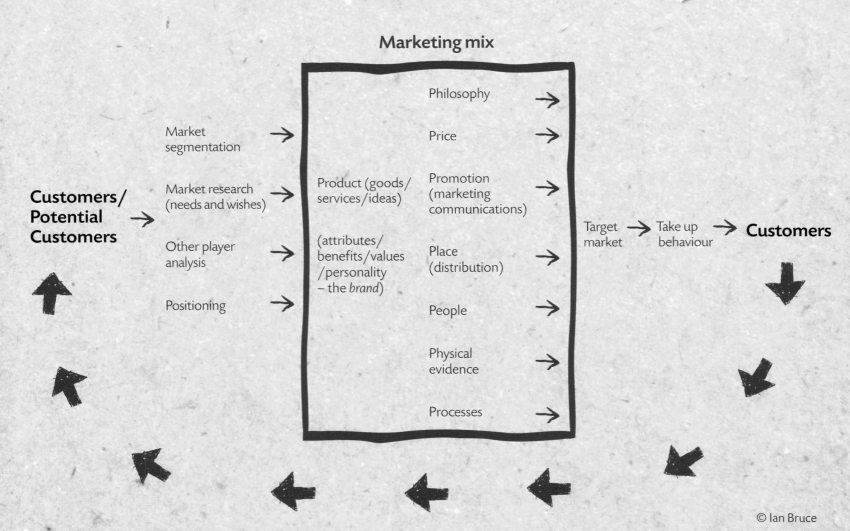

Marketing mix

Customers/ Potential Customers → Market segmentation → Market research (needs and wishes) → Other player analysis → Positioning → Product (goods/services/ideas) (attributes/benefits/values /personality – the *brand*) → Philosophy → Price → Promotion (marketing communications) → Place (distribution) → People → Physical evidence → Processes → Target market → Take up behaviour → Customers

© Ian Bruce